Belated Heavens

Also by Daniel Tobin

Poetry

Where the World Is Made (1999)
Double Life (2004)
The Narrows (2005)
Second Things (2008)

Criticism

Passage to the Center: Imagination and the Sacred in the Poetry of Seamus Heaney (1999)

As Editor

Light in Hand: Selected Early Poems of Lola Ridge (2007)
Poet's Work, Poet's Play: Essays on the Practice and the Art (2007, with Pimone Triplett)
The Book of Irish American Poetry from the Eighteenth Century to the Present (2008)

BELATED HEAVENS

Daniel Tobin

Four Way Books
Tribeca

Please direct all inquiries to:
Editorial Office
Four Way Books
POB 535, Village Station
New York, NY 10014
www.fourwaybooks.com

Library of Congress Cataloging-in-Publication Data

Tobin, Daniel.
  Belated Heavens / Daniel Tobin.
     p. cm.—(A Malcolm McDonald Series Selection)
  ISBN 978-1-935536-03-1 (pbk. : alk. paper)
  I. Title.
  PS3570.O289B45 2010
  811'.54--dc22

                                    2010001643

This book is manufactured in the United States of America
and printed on acid-free paper.

Four Way Books is a not-for-profit literary press. We are grateful for the assistance we
receive from individual donors, public arts agencies, and private foundations.

This publication is made possible with public funds from
the National Endowment for the Arts

and from the New York State Council on the Arts, a state agency.

Distributed by University Press of New England
One Court Street, Lebanon, NH 03766

[clmp]   We are a proud member of
          the Council of Literary Magazines and Presses.

TABLE OF CONTENTS

We see the external world of stars and four elements, in which human beings and all creatures live. This neither is nor is called God. God certainly dwells in it, but the external world does not grasp Him. We also see how light shines in darkness and darkness does not grasp light, yet one dwells in the other. We also have an example of this in the four elements, which in their origin are only one element that is neither hot nor cold, dry nor wet, and yet, by its movement, it divides itself into four characteristics, into fire, air, water, and earth.

Jacob Boehme, "The Fifth Treatise on the New Birth That Is," Article 13

I.   IN THE NEIGHBORHOOD'S THROAT

WESTWOOD

Yes, you think, it's hard to be homeless
even in the interval between homes,
the one you left behind a thousand miles
where your wife remains, unweaving rooms
into boxes piled with destinations—
Bedroom, Den—and the home that waits,
you picture, like a new Ithaka, its welcome
barred by land courts, capricious gods.
Of course, you tell yourself, it won't be long,
twenty days perhaps instead of twenty years.
Still it's hard returning nights from the job
to this house generously loaned by a friend,
under contract itself, stripped nearly bare
but for your bags and the one remaining bed
and the spindrift left of her parents' lives.

No, it's not easy to walk among remnants
of a lost world, even when it's not your own.
The antiseptic walker. The bag of shoes.
Shelves of kitsch. A jeweler's scale. Decanters.
Blunt inlays where the furniture would rest
bearing up beneath the warm familiar weight—
like casts of the rug's unalterable burden.
And on every wall an empty faded patch,
un-bandaged skin, where the pictures came down.
Whatever wound you harbor, with passing time,
seems less and less like Odysseus's scar,
that genre piece his nurse knew from childhood,
and more and more like the raging whirlpool
he pilots toward whichever way he tacks.

Though maybe it's better not to see the journey
as some insistent metaphor that surfaces
in lives that would otherwise be their own
instead of masks for the one storied life;
better to see the name of this suburban town
as an exit sign off the interstate
from which you will move on without trial
and not an allegory of your last end,
anyone's, or gulfs stretching between stars.
Now euphony wings through the barren halls.
Pick up the phone, your beloved is calling.

DOWN

The many naked birds, their bodies
released after the hatching and harrowing,
praise their patience, their stunned altruism
under the knife, the carcass's largesse
of softness, each under-breast a snowfall
suspended in air, each fallen weight

of eider inside this winter comforter,
all dulcet and lace where the lovers caress—
though not as prelude to making love
for they've grown bone-tired from the long day,
and want only this modest solace
where they lie now in their proximate skins.

What did they expect the doctor to say
in the white room with its pale, diffuse light?—
the lamp a barely audible simmer, a hum,
like the echo of too many years of sun,
its silent running of photons uttered
in cloud occlusions on the body's Braille.

Precautionary was the word he'd used,
and prepped each maculate interruption
along the man's back, then numbed, then carved out
what might become transfigured into flesh
that feasts on itself from the cells' hunger
as his wife waited in the outside room.

Let them rest like figures in a painting,
not the scene where the flayed god seems to float,
a feather from an angel's hapless wing,

down and down into the women's arms, but one
where dawn light christens them with dew
as if each numbered wound were gift, were grace.

INTRUDERS

I.

And then there was the one that streaked
from behind my mother's chair in Pearl Court
the day after she died, my father shaken—

*I haven't seen a mouse in this apartment
since you kids were small.* We gauged its wake,
as if it were some fleet-footed messenger

from the afterlife, or his love come back
(he seriously asked if it could be)
from underground, and the living room shook

with a strangeness that was palpable.
Inside of us a trapdoor had opened
into space—*Impossible, Impossible.*

II.

What to make now of this one—its unheard
sorties to the cupboard those nights we slept
and slept upstairs, like souls unburdened

of our bodies, until the clock-hand slipped
past its appointed hour, the alarm
jarring us back into our blunt routine?

Stray scat—apotheosis of the marginal—
lay in the Lazy Susan among the tatters
of cardboard and chewed plastic, so fragile

the coffered portions, the unguarded stores
of our lives, as though it knew our every move,
its disappearance assured by our stares

that hung suspended—no dash, no blurred sleeve
of motion across the floor, like a shadow limned;
or caught in eye-range like a last visit

from the newly dead as the old ones saw them
before they passed like yesterday's headlines,
griefless, into the gig lamps of what comes.

III.

You heard the pitched squeak where we'd set the trap,
and I came running when you called to find
trap, bait, and adversary gone, the raw snap

come down but the tracked body dragged behind
that ancient storage box—some broken cripple
with his cart hauled resignedly toward his end.

There he was, brown glass bead eyes looking up
at us as though we were gods, and we were,
his hammered frame caught in the clamp's stirrup,

his terrified paws scrabbling tunnels of air
when I carried him, trap and all, to the bag
whose wide, rearing mouth swallowed his fear

like forethought. Though forty years ago,
it wasn't him but me suddenly alert
to small eyes watching, vague steps on the pillow

that startled me awake, I think now, like a spirit
come in stealth to whisper the momentous,
then, turning back, thought the better of it.

FOUNDATION

Something there is—hydrostatic pressure—
that doesn't love a wall, or loves it too much,
an endless tongue of water licking seams
where stone foundation meets concrete floor.
All day I squat or kneel along a ridge
where gray base meets the foot-thick puzzle
of rock matched to shape and size, accomplished
ab initio by the stonemason's hand, his eyes
dark now as that incongruous slab
of marble wedged alongside granite,
and try to trace the fault-line of the flow,
sealant oozing slow motion from my gun.
The lacquer grows and dries, an opaque sluice,
while below water follows its longing
through another course or crack—

this middle element between earth and air
whose passion runs deeper than fire,
more subtle; though the ancients knew
it wasn't passion but process churning
at the bottom of things. Still, how else
to redress the primal flux, those currents
that were the dragon's tail of origins
lashing the ancestors? Give the brute
swell a name, *Tiamat, Drafn, Vijara,*
and watch indifference transfigure into will,
the god created in the creator's image,
itself creator—plush waters of my birth—
and destroyer—the suffocating tides
of my mother's heart, her lungs a raft
her body was no longer able to bail.

Once an ocean rose in my neighbor's bones
so high the parasite swam inside her eyes.
Once I stood on breakwaters at land's end
admiring shallows, welling luffs of waves
where later that day the storm surge reached
to sweep the boy under when his father
turned—a gray silence, and no body found.

I angle my trowel along a line of seepage,
it's double edge like water's hieroglyphic *v*,
a talisman to keep my ark afloat and dry,
though this slow flood would find the flow
in everything, would loosen the staid love
from stone until the surfaces poured free
revealing rock's undertow, that need
locked like denial inside the molecule.
I feel it too, riptide under the skin,
and like the old ones dissimulating
behind would quell it with my tongue—:

Don't take me now, gods of the cauldron,
despoilers, plundering tides, let me stay
a little longer here, on tangible earth,
kind gods of ablution and effulgence,
deaf gods of the hard world upholding.

AN ORANGE TREE IN REDLANDS

The green of its leaves—snippets
children scissor from a rain-tarp
for a class project, the bright fruit
an arrangement of rubber balls
painted this precise shade of ripeness.
And I'm like Thomas who would touch
before belief ignites his fingertips
with the slow dawning of the real.

No surprise, for where I come from
only tennis shoes grow on trees,
and the first islander to see snow
ran to escape the volcano's blast.
For you who live here, mornings
are this accustomed strangeness
rising like heat from the patio
and its scatter of Zoe's toys.

Though this tree's also a traveler,
the sapling planted from the grove
and the grove itself prodigal—
like chaparral, the carried seeds
scattering ahead of settlers
until they altered the indigenous
into a pristine dream. Time's an eye
that remakes the world just by looking.

I'm going to take your gift of sweet
globes in my hands; I'm going to feel
the skin's stickiness and sting
and split each one and eat it
and let it become me. I'm going
to make believe nothing is lost
in what blows on ahead. I know,
like you, the child's name means life.

UNSEASONABLE

Not much in the way of wind save the maples,
   wavery as though high on their own sap.
Close by, the last cricket on the street trills
   his one note homage to Eros and to Keats—
where are his *twittering* swallows? Not here,
   nor the languid god who betrothed his hair
to pastoral climes. A lone siren blares,
   coroner-crooner, in the neighborhood's throat.

Then again this freak heat longs to linger
   past pulse and archetype, would keep revving green
until the great orb burns prismatic, hangs
   like that CD disk on my neighbor's mobile,
tacked on the back porch of the universe,
   its songs locked beyond stone and tympanum.

WINTER STORM, JERUSALEM

February 2003

Not fallout, ashes, little nothing moths,
cataract spray of old wrongs remembered,
   gripes, griefs, that whirling blizzard of grudges,
     the gauntlet flung down like an avalanche

as the summit caves with a plosive sigh,
but this steady leveling of blown snow,
   the Promised Land a-swirl inside its glass dome
     as though an unseen hand had shaken the sky.

Now the prayerful in their competing hats
can relinquish their faces to wall and floor,
   their Gods elided out of metaphor,
     their longing swept to a syntax of drifts.

All things come back; all things go on forever
the desert whispers from its dream of distance—
   and this silent, white screen that falls like grace,
     like manna in the marmoreal air.

THE CAUSE

Unreel the human weave to molten stone
And still you'll find the upraised arm of Cain.

The hand that rigged the flesh in Abu Ghraib
Caressed another's for the feel of home.

INDEPENDENCE DAY, 2005

It's not the bombs
of light that thrill, big thumps
    drummed at us, time-delayed,
from our white-out war against the sky,
    but it's the shapes

    we marvel at,
pink and gold fritillaries, ascending
    flares that burst,
silver machine-gun asterisks of hail,
    rose, aquamarine.

    Another explodes,
and a day-glow cube races toward us
    as from some far off
galaxy—or is it just a huge TV
    flittering out?

    It's Christmas,
someone shouts, when a smiley face
    blooms red and green
out of the drifting fog of smoke
    that looks backlit

    like a movie set.
Now a glowing willow of sparks
    rains for what feels
an infinite pause before the dying
    cells revive,

re-animate
in what looks like whirligigs of sperm
swimming intently
for the Earth's darkened ovum
where they fall, fade.

On the river
yachts and cruise boats dawdle
under the show
safely awash in waves of flame,
while above a blimp

blazons Old Glory
in the digital clouds. Somebody
calculates each burst
amazingly for such effect
so we stay hushed

or cheer, or whoop
like the man behind us shouting *Yes*,
the mock love-cry
making some of us laugh,
in each eye

the same blinding
flashes that fury the skyline's
window mirrors,
as buildings keep standing
in a powder shower

from launch and barge.
Look: the last charges blast their tiger's face
        into the night
    as though we each were the tamer
        it lunges for—

        O I forget the name
of the mauled: Was it Siegfried or Roy?
        Behind us, a child
    screams into the bestial teeth,
        but only for joy.

THE SHRINE

In some countries, it has become difficult to rid former battlefields of land-mines since rats are known to drag them into their burrows underground.

Reuters

Down in their burrow under the battlefield
The rats have crowded, surging, ashen,
Spurred like a congregation of monks arrayed
For the secret rite performed by an elect
They know themselves to be, inquisitive snouts
Tasting the earth and its seepage of bones.

They hauled it here, dank temple underground,
Dragged it through grass risen from the dead,
Through soldier's blood, over Hide-And-Seek,
And the village idiot's shredded legs,
This pristine altar, hotwire apocalypse,
Un-detonated in the lift of air.

Deep in the hallows of the dim-lit hall—
A flickering of candles like slow fuses,
Incense, prayer-wheels, a procession of hoods.
Can you see the aura of the Limbless God
Hidden in the shrine's apotheosis?
Can you hear the harrowed chanting of the hymns?

THE AFTERLIFE

What's worse, nearly, than the nothing you hope it's not
Is the thought of your many dead still nearby
Watching you from behind your life's one-way mirror.

They seem as they hover behind the living screen,
So close you almost sense them in the play of movement
Glazing off your own form in a shop-front window,

Like the revenants of dogged film noir private eyes
Who shadow their suspect's every move, who ghost
Their oblivious quarry by blending into the crowd.

Over time, they come to regard your every intimacy
Until you're naked as a newborn before the afterlife,
The more so since you still believe you are alone,

That your solitude, even in your happiest moments
Spent with your wife or your remaining friends,
Can be unfurled, the banner of your inmost self,

Even if it's blazoned with the pretentious seal
Of your delusion. Is it their own failures toward you
Summoning them back to the un-resolving world?

Or what Agency do they report to with your foibles,
Mutterings, the wild outbursts of dread and dismay
You thought no one would hear, the unguarded rituals

Performed behind the closed doors they walk through
As if now were the moment they would make your arrest?
Though maybe they're only present like the part of you

That trails your life like a moon on a clear evening,
A new moon burning its absent reflection in a pond,
The light of its full face turned wholly to the other side.

LAWN THATCHING ON HOLY SATURDAY

Already tomorrow's backache
runs its insistent tendrils
along my spine, though nothing
to lay me low—a good stiffness
through which the body wakens
to its own fallible presence.

Like some antediluvian hand,
my rake's splayed tines claw
at the ground, garnering chaff,
last summer's luxuriance
swooned to a gray waste,
my lawn nearly bleached of green.

Here and there these several blades
keep their stubborn faith in earth,
flush as Whitman's disposition
while the thatch-bag blooms heavier
with its nearly weightless charge,
ragged as the dead poet's beard.

Too easy to say nature's enough,
like my friend last night over pints,
"When you're dead you're dead, that's it,"
his withered eye glazed to marble
where the nerve died, his legs
a topography of clots and sores.

Too hard to appease the wish for more:
this page the wind must have swept
from some child's pack—*Trace the Words*

and Color the Picture—braced against
my yard's border of evergreen,
a lost design, a blanched wing flapping:

really a flat Easter egg with clouds
un-shaded, a pair of eyeless doves
flying over—are they rainbows
shell-colored still? Down the center
a cross with curved, uplifted arms,
its dotted *He Is Risen* left undrawn . . . .

Tomorrow I'll turn to the garden,
last year's ferns a tussle of lace
blanketing the bronze knobs
of fiddleheads waiting to unfurl,
clip the walk's spray of lavender,
shear the hollowed shafts of bergamot.

I'll twist the sedum stalks that cut,
clear under the barberry bush
with its berries like shining blood-drops,
its thorns pricking even through gloves,
then a faint shadow under the skin,
that subtle burning to be released.

II. FINE DUST SIFTING

ROGUE MADONNA

National Geographic Explorer

You swing through the broad high-branching trees
and what hangs from your breast, your stolen charge,
flounces like a rag doll clung to by a child
whose parents disappeared behind a train's

ashen door. You hover above, primate Eve,
as if what you hold could forever be held
past passing eons and zones occluded
by the pixilated boughs, the primeval

receding in an advent of savannah
to the long outering journey away
from your defiant primal stare, AWOL
as you are from your tribe, a savant

among your kind who's sensed the economy
of desire, how it burgeons then withdraws—
zero bubbled to zero in the hoard.
You circuit the canopy in arabesques

clasping the dead thing to yourself, the rent
sock of your need that made the true mother
cry out, and made the others clamoring there
claw closer in common esurience.

What stuns us is not your anxious grasp,
the days of your body's failure to nurse
so the earnest TV voice encourages,
but your pause in a kind of grim stillness

there on the limb limned by the camera's
omniscient eye, playing at the source,
the limp body fed from your barrenness.
Still, an image like some immaculate mirage

floats to mind with its flawless human face,
a radiant All-Mother gazing at us,
past us, toward some distant *Ignis*
that gathers everything into its brilliance—

we your wilier cousins, you, the living stones.
And the child on her lap also gazing out
who will die in an ecstasy of tortured
flesh, a plump icon already cognizant

of this cosmos born in waste and burials.
And you looking back, one of the going facts
beheld in your beholding as though transfixed
by the low verdant tremor of the bells.

THE EXECUTIONER'S MEMOIRS

hold fourteen notebooks,
two thousand pages,
three-hundred and ninety-five

heads, each one
expertly ex-
cised from the body's

fluent text, the steel
honed as ice,
his work charted

meticulously—
places, dates, weather,
names and crimes.

On one May morning,
Rouen, 1914,
Jacques the watch thief

was severed from
his trade. Just so
François the assassin,

1925, October,
who cried at the moment
the bright blade

descended, *Long live*
anarchy, death
to the cops, leaves

tumbling like coins
on the hats
of the exultant crowd.

And for forty years,
Anatole Deibler,
you were master

of your exacting
profession—*Meticulous
artisan of death,*

the auction called you,
*discreet to the point
of obsession—*

having followed
in your father's footsteps,
who had followed in his.

Pates, noggins, crania,
brain-pans, domes
of thought, each one

fell for you in the blink
of God's eye
into the basket,

until that morning
your heart
cleaved itself

while the rail hummed
like a razor along
the underground—

your eyes sharp
in the pre-dawn station,
your mind wide-awake,

imagining the next
numbered head and the train
to take you to your work.

TO ACEDIA

. . . like those who go down to the Pit.

Razor of nothingness, ash
Of soul thrice burned,

Thought with its armies
Of malice turned inward,

Pygmy soldiers
Overrunning the field.

Slay one, a hundred
Rise to kill in its place—

A thousand cuts, and blood
An endless fog pouring

From the dustbowl
Of the heart. Languisher,

Purveyor of afflictions
In memory's back alleys,

Worm oil, searing garland,
You hawk the cold fever

That burns, liquid nitrogen,
At the raving core.

If mind were a knife
It would skin itself for you.

If skin could think,
And it does, it would

Crawl inside and sleep
For millennia,

Stupor that turns
The bluesman's song to stone.

There is only the fear
Of waking to this fuel

Consuming itself,
Consuming others—

The void's pure verb
That grows like a diamond,

A coal-black diamond,
On the tip of the tongue.

BITTER SKIN

As though his palms were a *mappa mundi*
and he the studied explorer, watchman

looking back from the offing of his life,
he traces his course,
                                        the embedded lines
forked or flaring that elsewhere would be scars.

How he made it here, pilot of himself,
flames in the hand's puzzled approximation

of choices and years.
                                        And where it begins,
the hectic parchment spreading up his arm

with its flaking script, its ciphers of loss,

defines the boundary of each mulled regret—
no, his long stare affects the alchemist

who would figure gold the secret of this rust,
the flecked skin a fine dust sifting free,

in each flyblown cell a life he might have lived.

CONCHIGLIE

Thrilled, or oblivious, the meal bugs
circulate inside the pasta box,
for them the one true earthly paradise
hardly dreamt of in the provinces.

To have wakened into life
in the ecstasy of conchiglie,
each coin of fluent flour-paste
machine-cast, transfigured
into a seashell's perfect artifice—
edible trove, infinite loaf.

Do they hear as they slide
into the conch's sweet tunnel
the siren's song of an ocean
equal to their insect hearts?

The lid lifts, and out tumbles
the cosmos into a boiling sea.
Dazed survivors scramble
on their flatland's folding corners,
while a few flayed swimmers
bob lifelessly in the oil's slick.

And the one who managed to lodge himself
deep in the recess of his dream?
We'll let him stay, swaddled
in sauce, before we eat him,
corpse in a deaf ear,
like any eminence or god.

IN NEANDERTHAL BEGINS RESPONSIBILITY

Not what we were it turns out, the original
lowbrow, proto homo-sapiens, grunting their way
across stretches of tundra, receding glacial moraines,
their eye-ridges like opera glasses fused to skull;
primordial goons, goombahs, lumbering their squat
selves through sci-fi flicks; fur-haberdashered firbolgs
glowering, cowering in caves, artless, incapable
of symbolic thought; woolly-backed mammoth-heavers,
saber tooth's *hors d'oeuvres* with whom, for eons,
we shared this earth, their brains big as ours, just one
of many dead-end cousins whom we rendered extinct—
possible extermination—and did so quickly,
only a few thousand years, nary a single strand
of DNA traceable: therefore not us, not us.

THE EXPEDITION

As if the cutter ploughed
through icing and not ice,

such was the troubling sign,
though others troubled us:

wrenched climates, storms,
the wild unseasonable seasons—

omens the polls ignored—
before our eyes widened

at a tonsure of open sea
where the frozen pole should be,

the ice core melted to a future
fifty million years gone,

the mists rising in sunlight,
our small lives lying down.

FINANCIAL STATEMENTS EATEN BY RATS

Big numbers, small appraising hands . . .

Debits, credits, spread-sheets consumed,
the deft, anonymous sleights consumed.

No numbers, no fraud, no future
for the defrauded, since one needs
evidence to pinch
even the pettiest crook.

Nothing left but this black bullion,
these dots of blithe shit trailing
across the floor like decimals . . .

CLEAR CUT

From above it looks like
stubble fields, the harvest
scythed to a broad plain
of chaff, cornstalks
shucked raw, slaughtered.
But it's trees: rainforest
the size of Connecticut
gone, except the hacked
stumps, the stripped
and leveled shafts lying
as though blown down, or
slashed by a vast machine.
Who whacked them one by one?
Not us. The ant army
of the poor (who better
to blame) carts logs away,
the crumbs of extinctions
scattering behind, the rare
white tiger rarer now, while
the saw's dinosaur screech
seethes twenty-four seven.
Good thing we don't live
here, good thing we only
buy the posh armoir, paper
aggregated out of pulp,
though the sun's blades
spread across obliteration's
stunted vista, the same
as in our suburbs. Call it
Gouge Meadows. Scourge Acres.
And earth was all before them.

AN ICON FROM THE FLOOD

Sent from Troy, Alabama, September 1, 2005

I watch talking heads drone on about the saved,
hollow notes in an afterthought of wind
when the storm's done, though the ravaged
nearby you, nearby your salvaged town,
troop like ragged pilgrims to some central dome
where God reveals himself compassionate
enough, we're told, to die for us in groans
flaring heavenward, and blood and shit.

Nature and history consume the great—
that's old as the hills and clear as tar.
And here's another palpable cliché:
art is the bulwark of our fear.
Against North Sea surges steel walls drop,
so land's reclaimed, computerized gates,
the size of ancient wonders, keep
the ocean from the port; profit saved
from a city threatened to seabed—
limit gnaws at the bones of the lost
the way sins of the living will outlive the dead,
and the mind warping proofs of physicists
who envision portals beyond this present phase,
other universes, other dimensions
where we build anew without outrage,
have not launched us free of our terminal sun.

In news footage they come, thrown overboard
by wind, by rain, by flood, by race, by lack,
not the teeming collective of a *cri de coeur*,
but one by one, not the least emblematic.
Still, these bright shadows of the poor's distress

mark the gulf in our idea of home
that widens as the waters rise
to swell the wards, uncovering a shame
that shocks like some vast mural of the damned
churning in fresco on the vaulted nave
of a church become a house of the fallen,
or a fallen house fled by the desperate saved.

The saint in rapt attention at the Word
stands in the icon as on a rookery.
Beggar's bowl and flagon swing from the edge
for the pious to fill for his subsidy,
while everywhere the sky shines golden
into which he seems ready to ascend.

Nothing blemishes that comprehending glow,
nothing but what looks like shades of damage
from centuries of seasons cured and stanched,
though still the orb of the saint's halo
from which he stares, his soul quenched
by the ethereal, seems the coin that buys us
our redemption, or the calmest eye
in a storm of utter Light; still, there,
below, what looks a marled, brooding tide
floods up to the little chapel's door
and changes the scene to tragedy:
a man pleads from a world consumed by waves
to us, to each of us, with his arms lifted,
as though it were we who needed to be saved.

DOG

Black lab, runt of the litter, the one
    pet mammal allowed
in our house, and for just the week
    of her failed trial.

Manic, un-trainable, irreverent,
    she came with the missiles
of October and peed everywhere,
    everywhere shat, gnawed

our mother's couch legs, pawed to tatters
    the new upholstery,
shredded curtains, slobbered the rugs,
    barked incessantly

the gruff petitions of the needy.
    In her the thinned-out
blood of the beast, shadow to Argos,
    inspired a comeback,

those nips at the hand, her trickster eye
    turned upward, as if
begging permission of the master
    to appease desire.

None of which tells why we gave ourselves
    to the playful maw,
to the raw edge of that life we kept
    at bay, then banished.

SMART ANIMAL GORILLA

Koko, who calls herself "Smart Animal Gorilla," has learned over a thousand words.
A CD of her poems sung by a human choir is due for release.
                                                                    News Wire

A thousand words, a thousand sonic baubles
Koko knows, more than most of us
or nearly, who are her hairless cousins,
who hardly savor the supple vocables

of the language (from the Latin, *lingua*,
meaning "tongue"), as she sounds the silent
amplitudes, a flurry of pirouettes
from the soft pads of her hands, her fingers

shaping signs: her by now studied translation
from Modern Ape to Trainer's English,
while her kin diminish like Manx and Cornish
into the hellbox of extinction . . .

Koko, inscribe your elegies from the cage
for the lost forest, to the human choir
who've assembled in the studio's glare
to sing the primal notes of your name—

Smart Animal Gorilla, who writes on air.

III. FALLING UPWARD

THE AIR MATTRESS

inflates out of nothing
so nothing fills
this sealed plastic sheet

elapsed on ground
while its little engine
hums in motion,

all space expanding
with the driven sound.
And under ground

the turtle of creation
swims through time,
while on his back

the world's buoyant freight
bobbles in tow
below the firmament;

or it's the god sleeping,
his oblivious cargo
a lotus risen

from his bright navel,
the universe nothing
more than his dream.

Before the dream ends
infinity wings by.
The god wakes, stretches,

then dreams the next,
that floats like this raft
with its two dreamers

under night's tent,
O pale belated heavens,
and a low wind breathes.

GREAT COW

The Great Cow rests in her fulgent pen,
a mansion festooned with exotic wreaths,
flower garlands, a coronal snooding
her henna brow—gifts of the faithful
who file before her, bearing the rosettes
she loves to eat, unguents for her hooves,
and pay no mind to her ambrosial milk
(her laden teats superabundantly hung),
nor the scattered cairns of dung behind her.

Lick me, Great Cow, the pilgrims petition,
hobbling on crutches, trundled in wheel-carts.
Lick my hip, my ankle, my burning shinbone.
Lick my bunion, hammer-toe, in-grown nail.

How quickly word spread after the farmer's cure,
his rheumatoid knee slathered
one day as he squatted in the barn,
healing genuflection, the anguished joint
released from its burden of fleshly pain.
And how does the cow feel about the change?
Her great dark eyes watch all things mildly
from the heaven of transfiguration.

And so this zealous troop limping up the road
that I would join against my skeptic heart
to make my own hampered way to the goddess.
Great Cow, lick me, lick my afflicted soul.
Salve me, lave me, with your hierophantic tongue.

CEILING AND GROUND

Two Romantic riffs . . .

What the young man desired was an art
Of ascent, a psalmist's praise, and at night
Stars. What he received was this world, apart
From what he wished. And though he erred, he might
As well turn to his self-appointed task
As to a calling, the way a man shores
Up his ceiling's cracked plaster with a mask
Of perfection, his brush absorbed in moorings
Of ivory paint, to mime the unchangeable:
Cold firmament, captive sky. There's no breach
Through which the body might suddenly fall,
Unprotected, upward—echelons in reach
Beyond the cloud-life and each passing breath.
So lights. Camera. The poet swoons to death.

~

Surpassing boon of grass—*There is no death*,
Whispered proposition under God's breath
That slips away, a catkin from your reach . . .
The effulgent dirt into which you fall
Composes you, mulch of self—reverse breach
Of womb/wound into an unchangeable
That adorns itself in change. What moors
You now is nothing, an emptiness masked
By what is: desire's recurrent shores,
And the mask the face, and to see the task
Accomplished *sans* the seer. You might,
No longer being, be no longer apart,
Like light's pure metaphor infusing night,
An absence present, the perfect art.

MAPPA MUNDI

Oceans, continents—the planet as it is
Jumbled, as if the topographer's eye
Had glimpsed Pangea, earth-puzzle, glut
Of shifting plates before the known, the named.

~

Where is this penned ship heading, to what port,
Its sail billowing in a parchment wind?
Wherever, it will travel beyond islands
Of words, legends in a dying language.

~

Outland. Tuhubuhu. Ultima Thule.
Natives with their faces in their chests.
On the horizon the sea-worm breaches.
Blank eyes. Corkscrew tail. Prism of the west.

~

Goodbye spyglass, compass, astrolabe,
Sun rising in jets and setting in steam.
Alice charts her laser through the wormhole
But the life of the leaf eludes the leaf print.

PETITIONING THE AIR

Mind beyond mind, word beyond speech, it is gathered
by no discourse, no intuition, no name . . . .

Absolute balloon,
cynosure, divinity
eternal, forever
grant humility.

Infinite *jouissance*
—koan, lover—
miraculous nothing,
open plainly.

Querulous radiance,
Shekkinah, Tetragrammaton,
unveil (vine / wine)
xenially

Yourself:
Zero Zenith.

THE HOURS

After "Les Très Riches Heures du Duc de Berry,"
Illuminated manuscript, 1410–1416

Like dancers in a pirouette
   the mowers with their scythes,
their polished rhythms whispering
   through harvest's green ballet.

Two women turn the tumbled hay,
   so slight and stocking-less and lithe
one could wish the world this script,
   no hail of brightness perishing

through blue that seems to radiate
   with morning light abiding
in June's long, languorous, florid days
   before the stars tip toward the Scales.

Above the town a gold dome wheels,
   though it appears unending flight
has stilled, just where the naked Twins
   pivot on the Crab's gilt depths.

A shadow God who bears the sun
   inside the sky-chart's inner vault
remains the still point of this route,
   beholding nothing but his gem

and innocent of these lives below
   as we are blind to any plight
behind the city's towered walls,
   no hint of plague or poverty,

for here is immanence and bliss
    and work transfigured into dance
the hours bless inside this cage—
    the gloaming fringes of the page.

THE WHEEL

I am content to live it all again . . .
Yeats

A pilgrim pitched along the blind, human track.
The stoned soul mired in its ghost-life of needs.
Who in their right mind would want to come back

To the self and its burdens, thoughts like bees
That fashion the teeming comb and its hive,
The stoned soul mired in its ghost life of needs?

Earthworms, galaxies, microbial lives
(Those migrant laborers under the skin)
All fashion the teeming comb and its hive

With hunger abounding—don't call it sin:
It's the grinding ache at the hub of sense.
Those migrant laborers under the skin,

You feel them at their chores, an emergence
You'd name, if you could—a wandering wish—
This grinding ache at the hub of sense,

This char that would become the radiance
You'd name, if you could. He wanders, a wish,
That pilgrim pitched along the blind, human track
Who, in his right mind, *would* want to come back.

A VOLCANO

Bartolome de Las Casas, Inferno de Marsaya, 1536

Above the white-hot core the pure sky burns,
A cloud-range back-lit in sulfur and gold.
What truth endures beneath the flaming stream?

In seething ships the Africans come in streams
Like Christ to take the place of those who burn—
The flayed, native skin that is the conqueror's gold

The priest hoped to save, for love of God not gold,
Though blood runs through time like a molten stream.
He watches from his perch the earth's offing burn

Gold, black, and red. This world's the burning stream.

GIORDANO BRUNO IN FLAMES

Burned at the stake, February 17, 1600

A breeze's aftermath of sizzled flesh
licked the strafed cobbles of Campo di Fiori,
    bore on its serpent's back winding through brush
the last whiff of Bruno, heretical meat.

Four centuries have burned, each one a wick,
consuming its essence like kerosene
    since your screams—you must have screamed—erupted,
and the Roman dogs picked over your bones.

Born in the foothills of Vesuvius
with the *ouroboros* beside your crib,
    you died having swallowed the universe
in your mind's feast of talismans and ciphers.

Old necromancer, numerologist,
for whom the One behind the multitude
    throbbed like a wound, there is no ecstasy
like the world-lust of those who murdered you.

Figures, hieroglyphs, principalities.
The body an aggregate released at death,
    launched to "innumerable living worlds."
And always at the center the Sun in stealth

dissembling in emblems, simulacra,
as though the code in each leaf were the name
    of the world entire, Botticelli's *Primavera*
unlocked from the stone mortar's mash of green.

They mocked you before they lit the fire,
"Italian juggler," though you saw the atom
    in the galaxy, and in their stares
your own charred finger pointing toward heaven.

    But you were neither magus, nor prophet
of this boondock earth, displaced yourself: a door
    through which we entered the newest orbit
between our desire and our solitude.

    On this late winter morning's solstice
I walk among my yard's reluctant beds—
    last fall's waste of leaves, mulch and crocuses,
the sun a white-hot rod boring through lead,

    burning its blank seal into the given
that I would learn to read, had I the art.
    O *res ipse, magnum miraculum.*
There is no center and love is at the heart.

PRAYER

There is something to be praised in repetition,
There is something to be praised in repetition,
For surely all life moves in seasons,
For surely all life moves in seasons;
Praised surely, for all there is—seasons, life—
Moves in repetition to be something.

Still desire for rest whispers in the body,
Still desire for rest whispers in the body,
Like the hint of a lost name or a nagging song,
Like the hint of a lost name or a nagging song.
Rest desires a name for the song, a hint,
Nagging, lost, like a still body in whispers.

Let me wait, a novice on nothing's threshold,
Let me wait, a novice on nothing's threshold,
Until the blown seed lifts on its diamond fulcrum,
Until the blown seed lifts on its diamond fulcrum.
Novice, blown fulcrum, let me lift on nothing
Until its threshold awaits the diamond seed.

Something waits for the body in whispers,
Diamond hint in seasons of repetition.
Or surely it lifts on a still fulcrum.
Let me rest, its novice, like all nagging life
Until desire moves, blown seed, nothing's name.
There it is, *Thresh-Hold*, lost song to be praised.

AFTER THE END

After the end the calm endurance of things,
As if life had lapsed into a dance of things.

What did he pray when all was taken from him?
To live at the pleasure of the chance of things.

He loved good books and inhabited their spells,
Believed they could cure his ignorance of things.

Once, dining at a restaurant on the coast,
He mistook heaven for the dalliance of things.

Race Point at daybreak, its tidal confluence...
Ocean blended to sky: the séance of things.

One is one, *mon semblable*, yet one is many.
O to live at the heart of the France of things!

The poet courted death; though what is poetry
But a line to get inside the pants of things?

Only a slave would mock Job in his distress,
His raised fist, his plea, his defiance of things.

Narcissus blooming, the secret he bestows,
To keep the mind whole inside the glance of things.

What he silently wished was what he most feared—
That there was no hope, no transcendence of things.

Daniel means "God's judge." His best self longed for God,
A home within the extravagance of things.

NEW MILLENIUM BLUES

I've been waiting for the sun all day
That's not so much behind a cloud
As the old bluesmen say, but the cloud
Itself: the gray, dead body of the sky.

The new earth's a ruin with sheen of gold,
And soul's what's left in the brass spittoon.
The soul's what's left in a brass spittoon
And the new earth bleeds as red as the old.

I'll have to wait like ore inside the stone.
I'll have to make my way like a seam through rock,
Make my way like a trickle through rock
Without a notion of the world to come

Till I find that ocean unimaginably wide,
Till I find that ocean but it won't be soon.

IV.   BOUND RAIMENT

THE GIFT

Who wouldn't, and I do, envy the diver—
rubber suit, flippers, transparent oval mask
in which his eyes must have burgeoned like balloons,
the air tank a torpedo strapped to his back—
who descended to these depths to find
lodged in the cartoon mouth of a conch, this emerald,
silver-dollar sized, worth a hundred million.

The waters, my friends, were not Wikiwachi's,
mermaids bobbing like nubile seahorses
through the bikini-infested lagoons
of sixties television, but somewhere further out—
Shark's Road, a flesh-rag in each sawmill smile;
hull-haunted tidescape where the smuggler's galley
went down, where fish picked their fingers clean.

It wasn't greed that spurred the journey—
he handed the gem to the fat-cats who hired him,
preferring his wage and a modest reward;
and though it was luck led him to the prize,
a gift from all the sea's secrets, it must have seemed
like providence, the deep's great, good word,
nothing ever, if anything, more beautiful

to come rolling, untranslatable, off the ocean's tongue.

AN ISLAND SPEAKS

Fernandea, a volcanic island off the coast of Sicily, could soon appear.
When it last emerged, it sparked a diplomatic spat over ownership.
Associated Press

Even now the dogged emissaries
are sailing to claim me with their flags,
though no hotels crowd my magma beach
above the bathing rich and paparazzi;
no tourist-trade and tax-base sustains
my place among the chosen of the race,
and I've made newswires if not headlines
for my curious proclivity to rise
from murky depths every century or so,
a minor Aetna emerging from the flow,
boiling skyward from the ocean floor.
Conceived in vents and fissures,
I am that primal thing composed of fire,
cooled by water, air, alchemied to earth,
provenance before any human birth.

A PALM PRINT IN LASCAUX

I.

I, too, want to reach behind the stone veil,
  To follow the rabbit down its winding hole
Into the whisper-chamber, bosses like sails
  Billowing in an earthen wind, this first world
With its presences recursive in the maze—
  Bison, ibex, mammoth, and stag, the steppe
Alive in limestone on the vaulted frieze;
  Down with my lamp to terra incognita,
Magician in my skin-cape conjuring beasts,
  Trove of the underworld's infinite hat.

II.

Tallow smell above the axial gallery,
  An island of light in the hall of bulls
Illuminates the surging cavalcade,
  As if stone had fixed itself from shifting clouds
Into these forms heard by the searching hand.
  Ochre hide. Black blooms of antlers splay
From a stag's head. Auroch's flaring horns.
  Something in the mind cleaves to this rock-face
Like a cave-bear's tooth housed in its niche,
  Scoured bones articulated in their graves.

III.

What hides, parietal, in the mask of dark—
   After-image the child fashions in sleep,
A drunk's tremens, a screensaver's bright mark,
   Virtual gallop across the humming screen?
As in a high nave curving heavenward
   Where the blessed pose in their spirit ride,
So these inhuman majesties surround
   The descendant. Flint-knapped, finger-fluted,
Walls move, tangible air. A horse reels, heaved
   Back like a penitent: the stunned, healed soul.

IV.

The wounded man recumbent in the shaft
   Awaits the bison's charge, arms outstretched
To embrace What Comes. Beside him his staff
   Floats in whitewash where an all-seeing bird
Contemplates a beast, tail-up, whose horned head
   Dissolves into the membrane of the vision.
Skeletal soul, mesne of the living and dead,
   First émigré to the haunts of the human,
Imaginer, your shadow runs like a brede
   Through the living coverts of our sojourn.

V.

Glyph-shapes, frescos, graffiti on their stall . . .
  On Ellis Island once I saw a hand
Traced in detention beside the Great Hall,
  Fingers flared like this one spit-painted
In the cave, an earth and breath communion,
  As though the negative of a child's print.
When the dying tallow lamp of the sun
  Burgeons to nothing and snuffs the planet
There will be just such a form to absence,
  A space left in space, immaculate—.

TO THE SNORER IN PENN STATION

It's as though you swallowed an espresso machine
So profound is sleep's cascade of hashing notes.
But your epic weariness doesn't keep the wiseass
Strutting with his girl from quipping he'll take a latte.

Nothing wakes you, not each blunt, blared announcement
For *The Southern Crescent* leaving on Track Nine,
For *The Northern Lights*, for *The Twentieth Century*,
Nor the bland commuter local to Floral Park.

What are you dreaming with your bags at your feet
And your Pavarotti body squeezed into its chair?
The vast stage set of whatever lavish spectacle
You believe to be world unfolding in your head.

Maestro, you will never hear these waves of crescendos
Unrolling triumphantly from the depths of yourself
As your audience shies away in amazed regard,
Your head thrown back, bravura, in the luminous hall.

LUNAR ECLIPSE

The distant band's just tuning up in the life you missed.

Even now it darkens, vaguely occult,
a patch slipped on by a one-eyed blind man
whose haunt throbs with song, raw, Andalusian—
the kind of discordant *frisson*
that pumps a healing shiver through the blood,
as if in spite of pain the earth were good
beyond plain reason. Up there: cloud-molt
clears like cannon shot, and a hint of red
blue-shifted in the shining. Would I could
take a funicular to the aureole
to find you in the innumerable lights
with the rest of the beloved dead, the Palace
of Memory brimming and the door un-shut.

Michael Donaghy (1954-2004)

WHERE LATE THE SWEET BIRDS

As though I'd summoned it with the word *behold*,
A starling flew from maple leaves that hang
Above my patio, green shade, and summer cold
As fall. A plane flared overhead. Nothing sang.
Jackhammers clanged the heart out of the day
While the sun arced imperceptibly west.
The bird scavenged before it flew away,
Scraps among poly-noses and the rest
Of what spring had rained down: lust's golden fire
To fill the earth with passing. It's no lie,
The wind with its sleight from *aspire* to *expire*,
And the wish I wished as the bird streaked by
Longing, in its dumb way, to make the thing strong—
The nest toward which it flew that will not last long.

LOAD-BEARING WALL

That morning when he lifted the faucet arm
in the bright kitchen with its view of a house,
its not distant turret vaulting like a wish
above the cross-hatched lines of winter trees,
and the un-thought, familiar rush of water
choked in the pipe's throat, he felt the ice
of his anger welling up from its source
in years of slow attainment and making do.

He half-expected as much, seeing his life
as pitfalls and obstacles, a turbulent course.
And could have predicted this latest travail
when his neighbors began the renovation
with a floor-shuddering hammer stroke
days before that inaugurated the plan
for more living space, more room, more light—
their dream of betterment: more of what he had.

Where they came from downstairs he pictured huts,
hoards of homeless in dirt lanes, their escape
one of an endless stream; though no excuse,
he brooded, for this thoughtlessness, this cheap job
he'd believed he'd find and did—pipes routed
and boxed against the shared, frozen shingles,
the new wall that would have to come down,
the wall that had and should have remained.

As he stood with them in the dumbfounded room
talking reason through his teeth, he foresaw
tense visits of inspectors, contractors,
raw exchanges in the common hall, lawyers,

the unkind cut of himself as polite victim.
That's when he longed for insulation,
for the lone house with its protected lot,
for the turret with its singular prospect

from which he'd survey his demesne, apart
and safe, though entirely magnanimous.
He saw himself there, but inside his thought
felt a wall come down and a view open
of vanished sufficiency, whole cities
of mold and spore, whole civilizations
on a leaf's underside, and each thing alive
on its shaking stem, its flawed resilient fuse.

FALSE SPRING

For John F. Deane after reading "An Appeal to Abolish War"

This morning in surprising light
Last fall's fisted cluster of leaves
Looks like earth's new growth, delicate

As baby's breath, the blaze of lace
On a wedding gown's frilly cuff,
As if bare limbs could change to sleeves

That waver in the wind's chill scarf.
The eye, unseasonable, gleans
Its wish—rose blossoms from gun-scopes,

A world more real in sibilance
Than scorn—but mindful of a stain
Like the mote at the root of a glance:

This sky's gray, unbroken stone,
The burden of tomorrow's snow.

SMALL ODE TO A SEA TURTLE

To travel rolling depths by smell
    and sniff the wind to find your path—
seaweed, beach-grass, spindrift of palm,
      such codes of the invisible

further you, mute current plodder,
    sojourner through muck and wrack-line,
ocean's navigator, parser
      of waves, tidal swales: old soul.

I knew you first in glossy pictures,
    then fed your image in a tank
in that room above the Narrows
      where I first dreamt of a future.

Nothing of your voyage compares,
    though I would, pathetic figure,
fashion you a simulacrum
      of my own bewildering desires.

And your port, Ascension Island,
    climbs from the littoral of words
into light bracing as blown surf,
      the shell of flesh become a raiment.

Patience is the art of all you've been.
    Sensing promised shores, you'll breach
into home's trackless air, you'll breach
      to nest, and to begin again.

GNOMON

O the hidden clock faces of Paris,
A la recherche du ciel perdu,
   Tucked away like ciphers
Where an obelisk's shadow measures the passing.

Say you've come to the City of Light by train
From the narrow life where you were born;
   Say you've come, withdrawn
From your own reflection, the given outgrown.

She who leans over to you in the night
Charging the crowded compartment with her scent
   Will remain the silent
Promise of the hours, the pivot point of flight

From which you'll flee, to which you would return.
You're a man scanning the blanched horizon
   For what cannot be shown.
A wind from nowhere breathes along your skin,

The atmosphere of a life you might have lived
Had the whim of occurrence been different.
   Alternate worlds branch
Like the wakes from a boat wherever you move.

Though the sky is clear in the life you've chosen,
A tree's gold leaf against a lucent dome.
   Forever one thing stands
Beside another. The heart beats. There is no end.

HEAVEN

You love the conveyances of getting there—
through realms of ether by fiery chariot,
by coracle across the Western Sea,
or latched to a flying elephant's tail,
the beast descended from Indra's palace
in that Urdu story. Like Black Elk,
you might suddenly be lifted on a cloud
above wide blue plains and piled mountains
to converse at length with stallions of the air.
Or maybe, as in some strange Gnostic spell,
you'll have to recite the secret names
to rise safely above the region of archons
who quiz the aspirant like border guards,
or bouncers at Zenith, the deity's exclusive club.
Maybe you'll travel alone, transported in dream
through porticos of light, so that everything
you've done or known or loved falls away
like shed skin, husk of self you leave behind.
Or maybe you'll ascend the scales with friends,
their names—Hopeful, Faithful, Worldly Wise—
refinements from the gray flux of your life,
so different from those earthly friends
who sustained or failed you, or whom you failed,
your denials dropped like crumbs on the path.
Or maybe, in your private *l'alta fantasia*,
Beatrice is the first crush you had at school,
Tricia Bardo, her name the perilous interval
the Buddhist dead endure to escape rebirth.
Though where she leads you—the awkward kiss,
closet games like "Seven Minutes in Heaven,"

78

the travails, failures, and short-lived conquests
leading to long love, sweet ease of middle age,
feels more like the journey you already made
than the one you will, the one you still fear.
How hard it is now to believe that nothing
isn't all after all, that there yet are worlds
where the dead convene in gardens or splendid homes,
naked or clothed in robes, or just in light,
and angels, their bodies unburdened of entropy,
couple for millennia with undying passion,
and where History, brutal allegory, evaporates,
so suffering finds redress, the starved are fed,
the dead reassemble in their new spiritual limbs.
At least let the last journey be like Reb Nachman's,
the celestial orchestra heard faintly at bedtime
until he wandered outside unable to turn back,
only to find himself sustained on air,
and no melodrama of souls whirling upward
in their frozen tornado of eternal praise.
Or let it be like that obscure couple
carved in relief on a cathedral wall,
among the line of souls the only two holding hands,
as though their mortal love persisted undiminished,
the Divine Life subsumed in their simple gesture,
and eternity were only a short walk together
to that still, small place where memory is healed.

AS ANGELS IN SOME BRIGHTER DREAMS

For Sally, who kept the shop . . .

Even you gone into a world of light,
Or some metaphysical luncheonette
   That smells in death of your shop's mélange—
Cheeseburger, brisket, baba ganouj.
   It's seven a.m. in eternity.
Egg on a roll, a doughnut and coffee…
   The ghost commuters queue at the counter.
You greet each with ethereal banter,
   Filling every want with foreknowledge
As you did in life, poised as Queen Noor,
   Magisterial behind your register.
Here at last is my Brooklyn beyond change,
   Moored and palpable as any mirage.
On the wall the cedars of Lebanon
   Flame green in a vale of whitewashed homes,
Your village limned by shutter and lens
   Into the split second of a sixth sense.
Had I grown up in your paradise
   Of biblical resplendence, an oasis—
judging by the photograph—from the desert
   of gain and loss, hatred, self-regard,
I might have stayed, believed home the reward
   I longed for, though I'd covet the promise
Of life exalted in a gleaming city.
   If so, time in the village that I'd left
Wouldn't be, in the great scheme, very different
   From where I found myself: the daily round
In a landscape of storefronts and row houses,
   Apartment prospects with their towers
Of skyscrapers across the teeming river,
   And that absence soaring above the harbor

Like a monument to anyone's lost world.
  If I sit here long enough with spirits
Of the neighborhood dead eating breakfast
  I might see against the iridescent haze
Of your ancient plate glass windowpanes
  My parents easing into their booth,
Regular as clockwork or ritual,
  Though they wouldn't see me, still corporeal,
On my stool-perch beside the chalk specials.
  How strange to know death made them happy.
How rich they'd seem like the others, Sally,
  Who look pleased this modest heaven is all
As they crowd in, ordering the usual.

NOTES

Westwood is for Martha Rhodes.

An Orange Tree in Redlands is for Joy Manesiotis, and for Chris and Zoe Beach.

To Acedia: More commonly known as sloth, acedia is one of the seven deadly sins and is closer in spiritual effect to clinical depression than to laziness. The epigraph is from Psalm 88: 4.

Ceiling and Ground is for Ben Howard: The "riffs" play bout-rimes with Keat's "Bright Star."

Petitioning the Air is after Robert Pinsky's "ABC." The epigraph is from a Gnostic prayer.

The Wheel: The epigraph is from Yeats's "A Dialogue of Self and Soul."

A Volcano: Bartolome de las Casas (1484-1566) wrote the first bill of rights in the New World. The son of a Spanish businessman who sailed with Columbus and a converted slaveholder, las Casas worked tirelessly during his lifetime to save native peoples under Spanish rule from genocide, even to the point of proposing Africans be brought to America to assume native labors—a position he later renounced. Thus began African slavery in the new world. This poem is meant to be read in the context of my sequence "Homage to Bartolome de las Casas," (*Double Life*, Louisiana State University Press, 2004) and completes that sequence. It should be placed as poem VII after "Utopias" and before "Protector of the Indians." The final poem, "Last Rites," becomes the sequence's coda.

Giordano Bruno in Flames: Giordano Bruno (1548-1600) was an Italian philosopher, cosmologist, alchemist, and priest, and an early proponent of the idea of an infinite, non-hierarchical universe, as well as the idea of an immanent God that subsumed the multiplicity of all things. He was burned at the sake for his heresy. *Res ipse, magnum miraculum* translates from the Latin as "the thing itself, the great miracle."

Prayer: The paradelle is a nonce form invented by Billy Collins as a kind of lampoon of highly repetitive forms. In the first three stanzas of a paradelle the first and second lines repeat exactly, as do the third and fourth, then the fifth and sixth lines are composed of all the words used in the first four lines and only those words. The last stanza is composed of all the words used previously in the poem, and only those words.

Heaven: The last line of the poem alludes to Czeslaw Milosz's epigrammatic "Memory and memory" in his "Notes" from *Bells in Winter* (Ecco Press, 1974).

As Angels in Some Brighter Dreams: The title alludes to a line from Henry Vaughn's "They Are All Gone into a World of Light." Sally's Luncheonette still serves in Bay Ridge, Brooklyn.

ACKNOWLEDGMENTS

My thanks to the editors of the following journals in which these poems first appeared:

Agenda, The Alabama Literary Review, The Alaska Review, Crab Orchard Review, Crania, DoubleTake, The Florida Review, The Green Mountains Review, The Greensboro Review, The Hudson Review, Image, The Kenyon Review, Laurel Review, Michigan Quarterly Review, New Orleans Review, Poetry ("The Cause"), *Poetry East, Slant, Slate, Smartish Pace, South Dakota Review, The Southern Review, Southwest Review, Spiritus, Stand* (England), *Tampa Review,* and *The Times Literary Supplement.*

"An Island Speaks" appeared in *Rhymes for Adults,* Somerville, MA: Virginia Reels Press, 2006.
"Clear Cut" appeared in *Outscape: Writing on Fences and Frontiers.* Knoxville, TN: University of Tennessee Press, 2008.
"Giordano Bruno in Flames" appeared in *Alhambra Poetry Calendar 2007.*
"Independence Day, 2005" appeared in *Alhambra Poetry Calendar 2008.*
"Prayer" appeared in *Alhambra Poetry Calendar 2009.*

I want to thank Christine Casson, Martha Rhodes, Bill Thompson, and Bill Wenthe for their help with some of the poems appearing in this book, and for suggestions in ordering.

Daniel Tobin is the author of four previous books of poems, *Where the World is Made* (University Press of New England, 1999), *Double Life* (Louisiana State University Press, 2004), *The Narrows* (Four Way Books, 2005), and *Second Things* (Four Way Books, 2008). He is also author of the critical study *Passage to the Center: Imagination and the Sacred in the Poetry of Seamus Heaney* (University Press of Kentucky, 1999). A book of essays, *Awake in America*, is forthcoming from the University of Notre Dame Press. He is also the editor of *The Book of Irish American Poetry from the 18th Century to the Present* (Notre Dame, 2008), *Light in Hand: Selected Early Poems of Lola Ridge* (Quale Press, 2007), and *Poets Work, Poet's Play: Essays on the Practice and the Art* (University of Michigan Press, 2008, with Pimone Triplett). Among his awards are the "The Discovery/*The Nation* Award," The Robert Penn Warren Award, the Robert Frost Fellowship, the Katherine Bakeless Nason Prize, and creative writing fellowships from the National Endowment for the Arts and the John Simon Guggenheim Foundation. Widely anthologized, Daniel Tobin is currently Chair of the Department of Writing, Literature, and Publishing at Emerson College in Boston.